Two Red Tugs

Story by Beverley Randell
Illustrations by Pat Reynolds

Two red tugs
Both work together,
Two red tugs
In all sorts of weather.

NELSON PRICE MILBURN

Once there were two red tugs
named *Keeper* and *Trusty*.
The tugs worked together
in a busy harbour
in all sorts of weather.

Keeper and *Trusty*
helped the big ships come and go.
There were large container ships,

there were long tankers,

and sometimes there were huge liners.

None of these big ships
could turn around in a small space.
None of them could get alongside a wharf
without the help of the two red tugs.
Keeper and *Trusty* would meet all the big ships
that came into the harbour.
They would work together
to turn each ship around.

Keeper would pull from one end, and *Trusty* would pull from the other.

Last of all, they would push
the ship into place
with their big fenders.

The two red tugs
were small,
but they were very strong.

And that was just as well, because,
one dark and stormy morning,
a big ship called for help on her radio.
"**Mayday! Mayday! Mayday!** This is the *Seaway*.
My engines have broken down.
The wind is pushing me towards the rocks.
I'm just outside the harbour. **Mayday!**"

Then, with a thump, she ran aground.

Trusty heard the call
and radioed back to the *Seaway*,
"We are on our way to help you!"

The two red tugs went full speed ahead
across the harbour.
Then they went out through the heads
to the open sea where the waves were enormous.

Trusty reached the *Seaway* first,
and took the long wire rope
that the ship threw across to her.
Trusty put the rope around the winch.

When *Keeper* came along she took a wire rope, too,
and then both tugs began to pull.

Suddenly, the wire rope to *Keeper* snapped!

What could the tugs do now?
Trusty could not pull the *Seaway*
off the rocks without help.

Trusty radioed to *Keeper*, "Come alongside.
My wire rope is very long,
and I'm sure it's strong.
I'll throw you the end.
We can **both** use it to pull the *Seaway*.

Keeper picked up the end of the wire rope.
Then she radioed to *Trusty*,
"We will have a better chance of saving the *Seaway*
if we wait for high tide.
When the water comes up,
it might lift the *Seaway* from the rocks."

At high tide, there was more water under the *Seaway*.
The water lifted her, just a little.
One behind the other,
Keeper and *Trusty* pulled the *Seaway*.
The long wire rope held,
and the ship started to move.

The tugs were able to pull her
right off the rocks.

But the rocks had made some holes
in the *Seaway*,
and water came gurgling in.

The *Seaway* radioed the tugs,
"I'll have to pump the water out
to stop myself from sinking.
I'll have to keep pumping as hard as I can
while you tow me to safety."

The two red tugs had no time to lose.
Together, they towed the *Seaway* carefully
through the big waves
and all the way into the harbour.

When at last the tugs pushed the *Seaway*
safely beside a wharf,
all the other ships blew loudly on their foghorns
to say, **"Well done!"**

Then *Trusty* and *Keeper* left the wharf and turned on their fire hoses, sending water high into the air to show how glad they were. They had saved the *Seaway*.